8 Pearls of Wisdom

A Parenting Guide: Empowering Children is the Way to Go!

By
Kimberly A. Morrow, M.Ed.

K.A.M.'S
BOOK PUBLISHING CO.

Copyright © 2018 by Kimberly A. Morrow

All rights reserved. This book or any portion thereof may not be reproduced or used in any manner whatsoever

without the express written permission of the publisher

except for the use of brief quotations in a book review.

Printed in the United States of America

First Printing, 2018. You may contact the author at info@Kimamorrow.com

K.A.M.'s Publishing Co. Los Angeles, CA 90008

ISBN: 978-0-578-41746-2

Forward

During my three decades of advocacy in support of quality, integrated public education I have engaged with countless parents of varying racial, ethnic and socio-economic backgrounds. The common denominator of these parents has been their want of a strong educational foundation for their children. Parents want bright futures for their children; they want to know what they can do to ensure the same.

In "8 Pearls of Wisdom," Ms. Morrow shares her stories of personal perseverance and triumphs from professional experiences encountered throughout her journey to support education, not only of her own, but for others as well. Her words are transformative B capable of turning the sands of uncertainty into a gem.

~Elizabeth Horton Sheff, M.Ed.

"When someone is taught the joy of learning, it becomes a life-long process that never stops..."
~Marva Collins

Dedication

This book is dedicated to my parents Doris and Earl Morrow; they were my very first teachers. As a teenager, I did not appreciate many of the lessons they were trying to teach me. As an adult, a parent and a woman who has gone through the storm, I finally understand. This is my official thank you to them for everything they tried teaching me, even when I didn't want to learn.

I dedicate this book also to my most recently deceased grandmother Marie, she was present at my college graduation, wedding and a mainstay at many of our family reunions. My sister, Kam and brother, Remarrow Morrow, who both continue to inspire me to walk by faith and fulfill many of my dreams, which include becoming a published author.

Furthermore, I am dedicating this book to all of the parents who have sought my encouragement, guidance, and inspiration as they work at being the best parents they can be for their children.

Finally, to all of my students past and present—each and every one of you have provided me with a treasure trove full of wisdom. I am blessed to share Pearls of Wisdom with parents around the globe who yearn to give their children the best life has to offer.

Acknowledgments

First of all, I want to thank God, my Jehovah Shiloh and Jireh, for protecting and providing for me through all the storms I have gone through during my lifetime. The source of my strength and joy has truly sustained me: In

1Corinthians 15:57, "But thanks be to God! He gives us the victory through our Lord Jesus Christ."

Next, I thank my dear friend Olivia with whom—along with two other dear friends, Stacie and Erica—I started our first business while we were all still students in college, called: "Just the Four of Us." Olivia, thank you for calling me every day throughout this process to make sure I kept to the writing schedule we created back in June. You are the ultimate accountability partner.

Also, a big thank you to my Mama Janice, dearest friends, Cheryl Larsen, La Ron and Dedrick Whitfield, Ericka and Matt Rohrbaugh, and Claudia Escobar, Debbie Rubio and each of you who stood by me as I went through my own personal storm, which began February 16, 2017. I am forever grateful for your love, support, and friendship during that trying time.

A special thank you to my family; Aunt Brenda, Aunt Patricia, Aunt Sand, Aunt Yolanda, Tiffany, Tasha, Shareese Reese Cup, LaTacha, Vernie, Rose, James, Sharon Tinker, my siblings, Vanessa, Larcenia, and Michael, and my nieces, Nitja, Khaila, and Kamani. Each one I named in your own special ways supported, encouraged, prayed for and stood by me during this arduous process. I am so blessed to have every one of you in my life.

A very special thank you to my cousin/sister Josina Elder, my original ride or die you have been there since the crib and continue to be there for me for all of life's ups and downs, I love you!

A special thank you also to my daughter, and soon to be writing partner, Kamaria for pushing me to write on my own and not wait for her.

To my sons, Brian and Brandan, always follow your dreams. The road will be tough, but as your granny used to say, "If it were easy we would all be rich!"

Last, but certainly not least, my partner, love and biggest motivator, Prince Watkins. We may not always agree, but your encouragement, support and love keep me going. I love and appreciate you so very much.

Table of Contents

Forward 1

Dedication 3

Acknowledgments 5

Introduction 9

Chapter 1 Pearls and the Number 8: Their Meaning and Purpose 15

Chapter 2 Pearl# 1 – It's Never too Early to Plan for Your Future 21

Chapter 3 Pearl # 2 – Taking a Leap of Faith 27

Chapter 4 Pearl # 3 – Have an Attitude of Gratitude and a Heart to Serve 33

Chapter 5 Pearl #4 – Money Matters 41

Chapter 6 Pearl #5 – Use Your Child's Interest as a Gateway to Learning. 47

Chapter 7 Pearl #6 – Diagnosis and A New Way of Learning 53

Chapter 8 Pearl #7 Be Your Child's Hero 61

Chapter 9 Pearl #8 – The Importance of Self-Care 69

Chapter 10 Extra Pearls 79

Online Resources 81

Works Cited 83

Introduction

For the past thirty years I have worked with students in a variety of capacities; as a volunteer at the YMCA, a youth director and coordinator in church, a substitute teacher, permanent teacher, assistant principal, and principal. In all of these capacities, I have worked with students from diverse racial, ethnic, religious and socio-economic backgrounds and one fact I have learned is at the core of every child is a desire to learn and achieve a modicum of success. No child is innately "lazy."

During my early years of teaching, I held this belief that it was my duty to save these children because they would probably never meet another teacher or adult like me again. Yes, back then I was young, idealistic—and a little embarrassed to say somewhat arrogant in a way—I thought in my early years of teaching. I was like other educators who mistakenly believed that parents of children with behavior issues could not possibly be interested in a child's educational success. How could they be if the child is coming to school giving all of his teachers and other staff members such a hard time? Therefore, I believed it was up to me with the help of a few other teachers who held the same standards and expectations as I did to educate and teach students appropriate and acceptable behavior.

I operated out of this misguided belief my first seven years of teaching. It was not until I began my tenure as a teacher in Moreno Valley, a school for at-risk students, that I began to change how I viewed parents of children with behavioral issues. Students with poor attendance, low academic achievement, and behavioral issues were recommended by school counselors to attend the community day school.

I immediately learned a great deal from the parents and students at Bayside Community Day School. First off, I learned parents of students with a history of low grades, poor attendance, and problematic behavior, do not want to be reminded daily by teachers of their child's shortcomings. Trust me when I tell you this, they already know, and they are just as much at a loss on how to handle the child's behavior problems as you are.

During my first week as a new teacher, I decided I would contact every one of my students' parents to introduce myself and acknowledge something positive about their child that I noticed during our interaction. I will always remember how happy and relieved those parents were to hear from their child's teacher with positive things to say as opposed to the usual negative reports. Many of the phone calls began like this:

> Parent: Hello (dryly stated).
>
> Me: Hello (upbeat and cheerful, the goal was for them to hear my smile), this is Ms. Morrow from Bayside Community Day School, I am "student's name" history teacher.
>
> Parent: (uncomfortable pause followed by) Uh huh or yeah.
>
> Me: I am calling to introduce myself and tell you what a pleasure it was to meet your son/daughter today. I especially appreciated his/her helpfulness, attentiveness, politeness, etc.
>
> Parent: (perking up) Really?? Thank you for calling I always get phone calls telling me what my child did wrong.
>
> Me: You can look forward to receiving many more positive phone calls, and if necessary you will get a phone call from me asking for your support on something specific regarding your son/daughter.

From that point on, the parents were much more responsive to my phone calls. I made it a point of duty to call parents as often as I could with positive things their children were doing therefore when I had to make the call for something less positive it was well received. Parents would say, "Ms. Morrow I know he/she must have done something wrong if you're calling me." One student reported to me, "My mom said, I know Ms. Morrow is not lying because she called me when you were doing well, so I know if she called me to tell me what you did she is telling me the truth." While working with parents of students labeled by years of documented at-risk behaviors, deadbeat parents became capable, supportive, and caring when they were included in their child's educational journey. Seeing this transformation by empowerment then inspired me all the more to incorporate parent outreach as part of my teaching philosophy.

I could not fully accomplish the outcomes needed alone. I needed the parents and they needed to feel included by me to truly support the child.

Over the next fifteen years as a classroom teacher and school administrator, I made parent outreach a larger and larger component of my work with students. I began to see the students' parents and the school as partners, and I strove to promote a positive working relationship with my students' parents.

During parent conferences, special education meetings, expulsion hearings, and school attendance meetings I would reinforce that their child's success is dependent on all of us working together as a team for the child. Of course, there will be a few angry parents that cannot hear the hope or the purpose while venting their rage, however, that is when I realized I needed to not react and allow my ego to get in the way of what is best for the child. Essentially, my inner battle to create hope is why I have been known to revisit conversations once the parent has had time to process what is happening and they are less hostile.

Transformational conversations are really a series; an entire episode in worst cases, of many unsuccessful conversations leading up to breakthrough and transformational change.

Results are dramatic. The most underperforming students rise to the top when they break to the pressure of parental caring that they change. When the child's ego gains attention from negative behavior, attention is redirected just as successful with positive praise.

I discovered this powerful process working as assistant principal at Apple Valley High School in a semirural Southern California school district. My reputation for working with parents, students, and staff led to my promotion as principal of a K-12 Alternative School of Choice in Apple Valley, California. Finally, I hoped I would be able to implement my vision of creating a Parent Empowerment Center for families of students identified as at risk of not graduating from high school. The Center would be a place to educate, support, empower, inspire and transform the way parents interacted with their children, children's teachers, administrators, and school district officials.

In the spring of 2015, as principal with support from the hard work and dedication of staff, students, and parent volunteers, we held the grand opening ceremony of the Parent Empowerment Center. The following year during our WASC (Western Association of Schools and Colleges) visit the team charged with extending or denying our accreditation did not only extend it, but commended us on having such a meaningful and powerful center for parents. It was the pinnacle of success from parent empowerment ideals I had developed over the past two decades of growing to believe this was the critical secret key to success with students where nothing else seemed to work.

On the heels of the success of the Parent Empowerment Center and after presenting to several parent groups in the greater Los Angeles area, I was asked to write a book sharing "my precious pearls" or in other words, the valuable lessons I have learned throughout my years as an educator. A book with the sole purpose of providing insight and advice to parents, students, and educators.

So, listening to the cry for an explanation of how to empower parents, I created this book: "8 Empowering Pearls of Wisdom that Provides Guidance and Support to Parents and Children in the Area of Academics." I hope you gain as much from reading it as I have gained from digging to the depths of my love for empowering the hopeless with hope in writing it.

"Pearls of Wisdom is the best accessory a godly woman should wear."
~Ruby Wives

"She speaks with wisdom..."
~Proverbs 31:26

Chapter 1
Pearls and the Number 8: Their Meaning and Purpose

In the Bible, some propose the number eight symbolically represents a new beginning, meaning a new order or creation, and man's true "born again" event when one is resurrected from the dead into eternal life. While pearls are a perfect metaphor for transcendence. This is because pearls are formed when a foreign substance slips into the oyster. It irritates the shell and its organ. From that irritation, a beautiful pearl is formed. That is the basis for choosing the title of my book. I see the number eight symbolically as a new beginning and the coming about of the book, which is as a result of various irritants (attacks) that have come against me in the years past. I truly appreciate this refining fire and the growth it triggered in me.

In addition, education is experiencing a shift that is not necessarily welcomed by all in the profession. We are living in a new age yet in classrooms across the United States, public education still resembles that of the 1950's, and it is worse for students of color and/or those living in poverty.

There are many reasons why public education in the United States continues to lag behind the progress made by other highly industrialized countries, which include racism, elitism, and one reason that crosses racial lines and which many in the profession will agree with; there are far too many teachers, district officials and board members that belong to a generation nostalgic for the "good old days" in education.

If I had a dollar for every time I heard a teacher say, "In my day a pencil and paper were all we needed," or "These kids don't need all of this technology. We didn't have it and we turned out fine," and my personal favorite, "Kids respected teachers in my day," I'd have enough money to retire to a private island in the Caribbean. Unfortunately, these are the people parents are entrusting their most precious pearls to every day.

The upper middle class who do not notice the hungry child is the angry child, not all ripped jeans are dress code violations, and a child that falls apart at that tipping point might be holding in more than most adults can imagine.

There is such a great gap between the socioeconomic status of teachers and a growing number of American children struggling with a myriad of current social issues.

Additionally, many of the parents are not equipped to question these educational professionals, who they believe know what's best for their children as well as have their best interest in mind. Therefore, I narrowed down the lessons I've learned and come up with 8 Empowering Pearls of Wisdom whose main purpose will be to educate and support parents and their children academically in a system that is failing our children. My 8 Pearls of Wisdom will benefit parents who are trying to raise their children to be kind, caring and successful individuals. An empowered parent armed with information will be able to transform their child's life allowing him or her an opportunity to excel far beyond their expectations.

After years of meeting with parents and discussing their children's varying situations, I have narrowed the areas in which they are in need of education and guidance. The main three areas are behavior, attendance, and academic achievement. Over the years, parents have expressed frustration over years of continuous letters and phone calls from their child's teachers regarding the above three issues. In my experience as an educator, specifically as a school administrator, I have learned that a students' chronic absences, discipline issues, and/or poor grades can be attributed to a host of other problems such as bullying, abuse, family problems, and one that accounted for probably half of my students issues over the last ten years, had to do with some type of an unidentified learning disability. As an assistant principal, I would discover after digging into a student's cumulative file due to my concern over excessive absences, a high rate of failure or numerous referrals to the discipline office that many of their issues dated back to second or third grade. Sadly, I got to know that this student now in high school had been a struggling learner for years which in most cases was a direct cause for the pattern of behavior he or she had adopted as a coping mechanism. The student may have been spared the years of failure, trips to the principal's office, and in some cases, a citation for poor attendance, had he or she been tested earlier to rule out or confirm a learning disability and given supports and modified instruction appropriate to their development.

Each new wave of educational reform pushes for "more rigor," "more University readiness requirements," and "higher test scores." Meanwhile,

Depression, Anxiety Brain and Emotional Trauma, Autism, Attention Deficit Hyperactivity Disorder (ADHD) and Attention Deficit Disorder (ADD) are on the rise. The growing divide between what the system expects and what the incoming children are capable of grows.

The lack of special education testing and follow-through could be for a number of reasons ranging from poor attendance, the school may not have seen a need for testing, or neither did the parents want their child to be labeled with a learning disability.

Whatever the reason may be, the child is the one who suffers in all of this. The child is being deprived of his opportunity to learn and succeed in school and beyond. The child learns to adapt to their deficiencies by a deflected attention away from his or her inability to read, write or solve math problems by becoming the nice student, class clown, bully, sleeper or absentee student. Regardless of the role, your child has adapted to survive, it has placed him or her at the risk of not graduating from high school and pursuing his or her career goals. Therefore, the purpose of this book is to help parents recognize the signs of learning disabilities and other problems causing your child to struggle, thereby pointing you in the right direction to get the necessary help for your child before it's too late. It also looks at the situation where the child is an adult, but still struggles to read, write, and solve math problems. Specifically, issues on how to get their child tested for a learning disability, accessing modified appropriate instruction, and the importance of school attendance. The link between students acting out in class and poor reading skills, and the steps to becoming a partner with their child's school teacher will be looked into. Also, parents being equipped with valuable and applicable information is not only necessary, but life transforming. The main question to keep in mind is what is this person going to do after high school and what preparation do they need to reach that goal?

The greatest pearl is when a young adult discovers their design and purpose; the innermost desires of their own heart. There is something inside each one of us that we love and will pursue with all our passion and devotion. This is the pearl of great price we are willing to sacrifice everything to obtain. In the Bible the Parable of the Pearl of Great Price, Matthew13 45 "Again, the kingdom of heaven is like a merchant seeking beautiful pearls, 46 who, when he had found one pearl of great price, went and sold all that he had and bought it."

New King James Version (NKJV). This is commonly interpreted in an eternal analogy to put heaven above all earthly pursuits. Yet, during our lives on Earth, we are designed to work and contribute to our communities developing our God-given talents and abilities. This satisfies our deepest need to feel useful and purposeful in life, as well as provide financially for ourselves and our families. Encouraging discussions for discovering your child's heart passions from an early age cultivate the ground for seeds of desire to grow into fulfilled dreams that yield fruit.

"The best time to plant a tree was 20 years ago. The second best time is now."
~ Chinese Proverb

Chapter 2
Pearl# 1 – It's Never too Early to Plan for Your Future

As an educator, I am often asked by parents, "at what age should I begin preparing my child for college?" My response is always a resounding, "NOW!" I will then follow up with an explanation of the importance of instilling career and college readiness skills in children as early as kindergarten. Parents should be exposing children to various colleges, careers and the professionals who work in these fields as soon as they are able to walk and talk. It is never too early to help children plan for their future.

As long as I live, I do not believe I will ever forget the day I was called in to see my counselor, Mrs. Maybloom. It was late spring of my senior year at Hamilton High School. I distinctly remember her asking, "Kim, what are your plans after you graduate high school"? At seventeen I was pretty much in lala land, and I had no clue what my plans were after high school. So, I said the first thing that came to my mind which was, "I want to be a Funeral Home Director. My uncle owns a funeral home in Arkansas, and many of my cousins work with him, so I'll just follow in the family business." She appeared to be content with my response and sent me back to class.

Years later, as a college student, I realized my counselor did me a disservice by waiting until the spring semester of my senior year to call me in to inquire about my plans after high school. I learned the hard way that those were conversations she should have had with me during my first semester of high school. There is a lot of preparation required if the career you want to go into requires college. There are classes students must take in high school to be University of California ready, and there are certain grades expected to be earned. There is also the Scholastic Aptitude Test (SAT) or American College Testing (ACT) required for entrance.

In the spring semester of my senior year, I did not know what was required to attend college nor did I have any idea "what I wanted to be when I grew up."

As a result, for the next five years, after I graduated from high school, I floundered around like a fish out of water trying to figure out what I wanted to do with my life and the steps I needed to take to reach my goals.

For many years, I carried with me the conversation I had with my high school counselor all those years ago. However, instead of blaming her or being angry with her lack of concern for my future, I made a choice to apply the lesson I learned into my personal and professional life. I used my experience as a cautionary tale for students, parents, and even my own children. The story usually began with, "If you don't plan early you could end up like me, bouncing around from one community college to another and/or one career idea to another." When I finally went away to college (five years after graduating from high school), I remember someone asking me, "What were you doing after high school? Were you in the military or something?" I chuckle now when I think of the question and knowing the answer was, "Or something." I spent the first five years after graduating high school attending classes, failing classes, getting kicked out of community college, working, dating, and partying.

That single experience has shaped my parental and educational philosophy on exposing children at an early age to colleges, various careers, and professionals working in those careers.

My daughter was practically born on a college campus. She spent her first year on the college campus of Morris Brown and at an early age was exposed to college students, college graduates, and college life. Once I became a parent, I realized all those years ago that it was not only the job of my high school counselor to discuss my plan after high school. Instead, it was the job of every adult in my life to help set me on my college and/or career path.

Therefore, as I stated at the beginning of the chapter when asked by parents how early they should expose their child to colleges and careers, my answer is always, "The earlier, and the better." As soon as children are able to walk and talk, parents should be taking them to visit college campuses, introducing them to professionals and enrolling them for activities around college and career readiness. The earlier your child is exposed, the better prepared they are.

School rarely fulfills this requirement as much as parents might assume. I also inform parents that there are some parents who are exposing their children very early in life and planning while they are in preschool to attend an Ivy League school. Those who wait for high school are already years behind many of their peers. It is up to the parents to instill college and career readiness dreams with on-going years of questions and conversation, awareness of realistic expectations of the child's ability and potential, and knowledge of finding resources to access the dreams. Most of all the parent must guide the child to discover their own dreams rather than impose their own. This requires the parent to teach and trust the child to think for themselves and to leave us to become who they are meant to be.

There are so many articles written about parents, mostly wealthy parents, who begin planning to send their children to college while they are still pregnant. They join elite baby groups, parent-toddler groups, all in the hopes of getting their child into an exclusive baby Ivy League nursery school with a plan to get them into an Ivy League college. *Town and Country Magazine* and the *New York Times* each have had articles written about the parents who are fanatical about their children's educational and financial future.

Recently, there was an article published on *Bloomberg.com* July 30, 2018, by Suzanne Woolley that is all about a summer camp for the super-rich. The article aptly titled, *Summer Camp for the Ultra-Wealthy Teaches Kids How to Stay Rich*. The workshops covered topics for all parents regardless of their level of income. They would like their children to know about such things as personal branding, philanthropy, and social entrepreneurship.

We live in a time in which access to information is available to us at the click of a key or command to Siri with our voice. We have access to knowledge and information unlike any other generation in history has had. The use of technology by parents to assist them in preparing their children for college and career can bridge many gaps for children who come from underserved communities. Parents can teach children about colleges and careers without leaving their homes. They can have their children video chat with various college professors and career professionals. These people can share their experiences and inspire future generations to begin planning early for their future. Many schools can also provide virtual tours of their campuses for parents who may not have the resources to travel to the schools for a visit.

Also, there are a number of non-profit organizations that specialize in working with low-income students and minority students. Check your area for local agencies that provide enrichment programs for the youth. In many states, you can check with the local chapter of the Boys and Girls Club, Young Men's

Christian Association (YMCA), National Association Advancement of Colored People (NAACP) and 100 Black Men of America.

As a direct result of my experience with poor planning, I have made it a top priority to routinely expose students to colleges and careers regardless of their age, their grade point average or their family's economic circumstance. Over the years, I have successfully introduced students to Historical Black Colleges and Universities, Ivy Leagues such as Harvard, and the Sorority and Fraternity lifestyle. I will continue to do this because I know firsthand how difficult it is when one fails to plan their future early.

S.M.A.R.T Goal Setting

What does SMART goal or S.M.A.R.T goal mean? S.M.A.R.T. is an acronym meaning:

S - Specific, Significant, Strategic

M - Measurable, Meaningful, Motivational

A - Attainable, Achievable, Adjustable

R - Relevant, Realistic, Results

T - Timely, Tractable, Tangible

EXAMPLE: A general goal would be, I want to lose some weight. A specific goal would be, I want to lose 10 pounds in 2 months and I will eat properly and exercise at least 3 days a week to accomplish my goal.

Identify at least 3 short term goals and one long term goal. Goals could be personal, academic or even involve traveling.

Short Term Goals

1.

2.

3.

Long Term Goals

1.

2.

3.

"Faith is taking the first step, even when you can't see the whole staircase."
~Martin Luther King Jr.

Chapter 3
Pearl # 2 – Taking a Leap of Faith

Parents, more times than I can count, I have told the following story to my students and their parents about my educational journey. My journey began in February 1990 while I attended a Historically Black Colleges and Universities (HBCU) at El Camino College where I was attending for the second time. I first began going to El Camino College after I graduated from high school. Since I did not have a plan, I let my cousin convince me to drive all the way to Torrance to go to school with her. After two years of barely showing up to classes because my preference was to hang out in the student center playing cards and listening to music, I received notice at the end of the spring semester in 1987 that I was being "kicked out" or as they put it, "Academically Dismissed."

Afterward, I decided to attend West Los Angeles College which was closer to my house. My cousin was in a singing group and she had already stopped going to El Camino to pursue her singing career, traveling to Korea at this time, so it was no big deal going to West LA College. I still had my poor study habits, and I still majored in my social life; I loved to go out with my girlfriends. So, at this time, I was placed on academic probation. Thankfully, before they had a chance to academically dismiss me, I had re-enrolled at El Camino College again.

So, there I was, the last day in February, talking to a visiting recruiter from various HBCUs, when I made the life-changing decision, right then and there, to apply. I didn't have the grades or the credits, but I was ready to make a move, and that is exactly what I did. I was accepted to Grambling and Morris Brown College. I decided I would go to Atlanta, since as my brother said, "You're from a big city, you won't like being in a small town." So, off to Atlanta I went. I didn't have the grades or credits to apply as a transfer student. I didn't have the money, and I didn't have family or friends in Atlanta. But, I didn't let that stop me.

People often ask me, "What made you go to Atlanta by yourself? How did you have the courage or strength to do what you did?" I tell them sometimes in life you must take a leap of faith. You have to put your trust in God.

I applied to four colleges, despite my current grades or the number of credits I had, and I received two acceptance letters. I encourage students and parents to support their child in pursuing their dreams even if you have failed over and over, because what if this is the time you do make it?

Each day that we get up and get out of our beds we are taking a leap of faith. We are believing that we will make it to our destinations and we will make it home safely. Just getting up and leaving the house is a leap of faith because we never know what can happen when we walk outside of our door. We are not promised a safe departure or return. Accidents can happen at any time, during the day anything can happen to us while we are out. Therefore, having that perspective makes it easier to take bold steps and calculated risks. I'm not suggesting you just go out there and throw caution to the wind, but there are sometimes when you cannot overthink a situation, and you just have to trust that the decision you are making at that given moment is the right decision. Listening to your own gut about what you want and going in that direction are critical to success.

My decision to leave the city where I grew up, my apartment I shared with my childhood friend, and the security of my parents was the best decision I ever made for myself.

I had the best experience in Atlanta and at Morris Brown College. My first day there I met the girl who would later become my roommate and best friend, Stacie. Stacie and I clicked the moment we met. She was and still is larger than life. She has an outgoing personality that immediately draws people to her. She reminded me of a full-figured Jackee Harry from the 80's hit sitcom *227*. Stacie was the opposite of the standard of beauty I had grown up with. She's brown-skinned, short haired, and a plus size woman. But, she attracted the attention of men any place we went with her curves and enigma. About a month later I met two other girls that would eventually become my best friends and would complete our sisterhood circle.

While matriculating at Morris Brown, I felt like it was my second chance at getting involved and taking academics more seriously. In high school, the only club I joined was the French Club. I also still was not the best student academically. I also never felt a connection to my classmates. I loved Junior

High School because I had so many friends. I was in Drill Team, so on the weekends, I hung out at the World on Wheels skating rink, the Fox Hills Mall, the movies, and house parties. My friends were the best friends one could have. I was voted Most Sociable in Junior High School. When the time to choose a high school came, most of my junior high classmates were planning to go to Palisades High School. Since I had ridden a school bus for the past four years, I refused to ride one for the next three years, so, instead of going to high school with the majority of my friends, I opted to go to Hamilton High School. Morris Brown was my do-over.

I got involved in the school in a way I never did while in high school. I felt a strong connection with my classmates, professors, and the administration. I participated in the storming of the school President's residence when our heat went out during one of the coldest winters in Atlanta. I stepped outside of my comfort zone and competed in Miss Black and Gold Pageant sponsored by Alpha Phi Alpha fraternity. I became an Alpha Sweetheart and an Alpha Kappa Alpha. My girlfriends and I even started our own sandwich business which we marketed to the staff on campus and which we named "Just the Four of Us."

Another college achievement was when I went to Washington D.C. as a delegate for the Model Organization for African Unity, and I helped write the History section in the *Morris Brown Catalog* for 1994. The best part of my time at Mortis Brown College was, I graduated! I graduated in four years.

Now during my time at Morris Brown, I met and fell in love with another student from Howard University. He graduated three years earlier and during that time we had a daughter. But, I still graduated.

My confidence grew tremendously while I was a student and I learned how to be a true independent woman. None of which would have happened had I not taken that leap of faith and gone to Morris Brown College. Although, I had no family or friends there, and didn't know how I was going to pay for my degree, I still made the move.

I had my ups and downs while I was there. I was homesick, I had some girls threaten me, and I had my share of broken hearts while I was a student. But nothing compares to all the blessings that came my way. The friends I still have and the experiences I gained cannot be quantified nor taken away from me. When it comes to my decision to take a leap of faith, I would do it all over again. I have absolutely no regrets when it comes to my time spent away at college.

If you have the opportunity to take a leap of faith, I say do it! Do not let fear stop you from pursuing your desires. I believe God has written the deepest desires into our hearts and wants to fulfill them. Besides if you have faith, fear cannot win.

Jesus told his disciples when they asked him, "Why couldn't we cast out the demon?" "You don't have enough faith," Jesus told them. "I tell you the truth, if you had faith even as small as a mustard seed, you could say to this mountain, 'Move from here to there,' and it would move. Nothing would be impossible." Matthew 17: 19-20.

You don't have because you don't ask. So many times, we limit ourselves with untrue faulty thinking about how this universe works and fall short of our design and purpose.

Parents, it is important to teach children early on the dangers of allowing fear to paralyze them from making what could be a life-changing decision. It is vital for children to learn early to have faith but let them not confuse having faith with being foolish, as there is a difference between the two.

One such example occurred years ago while I was an assistant principal. I had a parent who insisted her son attend a four-year college, although he was not academically, emotionally, or socially prepared. He did not have the required courses to attend a state college or UC and his grades and follow-through simply were not there. Although he was outgoing, respectful and could virtually talk his way out of most situations, he was not successful in his first year of college. My recommendation to his parents was that he attend a community college for his prerequisite classes. This would allow him to build up his study skills while learning to become self-disciplined and self-motivated.

I met with the student whom I will refer to as "Kyle" after his first semester and inquired regarding how he was doing in school. His reply was reminiscent of all the times I questioned him about his classes while he was in high school addressing his excuses. "The teacher made a mistake on my grade. I'm going to have to talk to him about it when I get back to school." All I could do at that point was offer a few words of encouragement. I realized he was not ready to hear the truth. So, I made a choice. Rather than be negative, I kept a positive outlook. I later learned that he did not do well second semester either. He was academically dismissed from the school. That was during the 2011/2012 school year, and six years later he is still trying to find his way.

Getting off to a realistic right start with supports and consequences that don't allow for excuses is a critical foundation for success.

There is nothing wrong with being a late bloomer, however, it is important for a parent to know when to encourage and when to be realistic regarding the child's capabilities, strengths, and weaknesses. If there is any doubt about the child's success in career and/or college, seek support from the school, local and state agencies, or non-profit organizations. Most people want all children to be successful. contributing members of society. Students who are contributing members of society are less likely to commit crimes and are more likely to pay taxes, vote, and serve their community.

> *"There are many talented people who haven't fulfilled their dreams because they over thought it, or they were too cautious, and were unwilling to make the leap of faith."* - James Cameron

"Gratitude and service are the two best paths to joy. I mean, I'm not stupid-if you want loving feelings, do loving things. Period."
~Anne Lamott

Chapter 4
Pearl # 3 – Have an Attitude of Gratitude and a Heart to Serve

On more than one occasion, I have had students confide in me about their troubled home life. I have heard so many horror stories ranging from physical, verbal, and sexual abuse, neglect, and poverty. There have always been one or more incarcerated parents. During many of these conversations, my goal is to speak life into my students. I tell them that while I have had a number of my own personal tragedies and experiences, I have not had yours. I too am the typical educator.

In addition, to recommending they speak with a licensed counselor or therapist, I also suggest they participate in some type of community service. Anytime we can focus on someone else's problems, it takes our mind away from our own problems and situations. Helping others is actually healing and therapeutic, or at least it has been for me, and for many of my students I have suggested they do this.

Which is why I began recommending to all of my students and their parents find a way to serve others. It is important students learn at an early age not to become self-absorbed. They also need to know they are not the only person experiencing pain or hardship in life. Focusing on others can also be an empowering attempt for young people and children because it places them in a position of being someone offering help and not someone who is always in need of help from others.

A few years ago, we had a student who was not very nice at all. He was arrogant, spoiled, and condescending to his counselor and me. He was behind in credits, and so his counselor recommended he attend summer school.

Being the entitled spoiled brat, he was, he showed up late to register for the class he needed. The class was full by that time, and he was unable to enroll for summer school. He and his mother became belligerent and accused us of being racist towards Mexicans and stormed off threatening to file a complaint against us. However, no complaint was ever filed, and when the student returned in August, he was a completely different person. When I spoke to him, he was thoughtful, respectful, and exuded kindness. I sat in disbelief because this was most certainly not the same young man who left here in May.

I decided to ask what sparked this change in him. He shared with me that over the summer he had volunteered at the animal shelter in an attempt to gain the credits necessary to graduate on time. He admitted that when he first began, it was just a means to get credits. However, the experience ended up being a transformative experience for him. He told me that seeing how people had mistreated these animals opened his eyes in a way that no one could have ever done.

The extreme change of character happened by simply telling him about the horrors. He said, seeing the abuse the animals had suffered and how they continue to suffer made him realize he had a lot to be thankful for in his life.

He also shared that the experience caused him to look at himself and how he treated others.

At the end of our conversation, he said to me, "I realized while volunteering at the animal shelter and seeing how hurt the animals were, I could never be the person I was before ever again and mistreat others.

This experience made him kind, compassionate, caring, and responsible. "Seeing the animals' pain helped me understand that I have to be a better person and so I am," he explained.

I am happy to report that the young man lived up to his word. I never again saw the spoiled, entitled brat that I saw during his junior year. That experience changed him for the better, which is why I highly recommend to parents and guardians of children who are either going through problems at home or have become a spoiled, entitled brat to focus on service and gratitude.

How many times have you found yourself complaining about your problems or your lack of money or other resources? Well, do not beat yourself up! Many parents—including me—have found themselves complaining about money problems and/or family issues. Our children see us doing this and they emulate us. Which is why it is critical for us to demonstrate to our children at an early age how to have an attitude of gratitude.

What does it mean to have an attitude of gratitude? According to LaDonna Greiner the author of the book series, *21 Reasons to Say Thank You*, and the website with the same name, she states:

> An attitude of gratitude means:
>
> You approach life with gratefulness. Focus on the aspects of an event, situation or occurrence. Choose to view things that happen in life with optimism, grace, and forgiveness. Find constructive ways to use incidents in life.
>
> It's considering those who help you and thank them.
>
> It's appreciating the things you have and those who made them possible.
>
> It's practicing positive self-talk that encourages and affirms, instilling confidence in yourself and the future.
>
> An attitude of gratitude leaves no room for fear, greed, hate, negativity, bitterness, selfishness, mean-spiritedness, anxiety, regret, self-loathing, animosity, pessimism, cynicism or any other malicious or destructive behaviors.
>
> Anyone can develop an attitude of gratitude.
>
> Everyone can benefit from gratitude.
>
> Start Today!

Children who practice an attitude of gratitude are more likely to develop a heart to serve as well. Learning to be grateful for what you have tends to allow less time to focus on the things you are lacking. In addition, the more you show gratitude, the less stressed you will be, and the happier you will become.

Years ago, after watching an episode of Oprah in which she recommended having a gratitude journal, I began keeping one. Initially, it felt forced to say how thankful I was for small things like having water to drink, or a roof over my head or clothes to wear. However, when I realized I was complaining about first world problems, it made me genuinely appreciate and be thankful for everything I did have.

After that, I began to encourage my students to do the same when they felt as though everything was bad or going wrong in their lives. Even my students who have suffered trauma, abuse, neglect, or poverty still had something or someone to be thankful for and appreciative of. Sometimes it was a challenge to get them to focus on what was good in their life, but eventually, they were able to do so.

One student I remember very well had been abused, her father was incarcerated, and her baby's father was in and out of juvenile hall. We talked on several occasions since she was sent to my office often for her disruptive and defiant behavior toward the teacher.

I explained to her there was another way to look at her situation. One day she will be in a position to share with other girls how difficult it was for her, but how, despite her difficulties and challenges, she still found a way to graduate high school and continue to pursue her education for the sake of her child.

I also pointed out to her that instead of focusing on all of the bad things that have happened to her, she should start focusing on the good things, like her son. I told her that while I can relate to students who have experienced the loss of loved ones or family members with mental health issues, I have no personal knowledge of what it is like to have a parent incarcerated or to be abused by a relative or foster parent responsible for my care.

I asked her to think of it as being placed in this terrible situation so that one day she could use her story to inspire others. But, first you have to graduate and do something with your life so that you can use yourself as an example to those who are going through what you went through. If you give up, you will deprive some other girl of your story and how you were able to overcome your challenges.

To my greatest relief, I was able to get through to her, and she actually began to keep a gratitude journal of her own.

The day she graduated high school she thanked me for always supporting and encouraging her. She told me, "I want to be a social worker so that I can help other girls who are in my situation." I was so proud of her. I am optimistic that she was able to accomplish her goals and is somewhere today working with girls who resemble the girl she was.

I have not seen her since she graduated high school since she was required to leave her foster home after graduation. I am grateful I had the opportunity to work with her and inspire her to focus on the positive things in her life.

Gratitude Journal

Things I Am Grateful for Today:

1.

2.

3.

4.

5.

6.

7.

8.

9.

10.

Things I am Grateful for In the Future:

1.

2.

3.

4.

5.

6.

7.

8.

9.

10.

*"You can only become truly
accomplished at something
you love. Don't make money your
goal. Instead, pursue the things
you love doing, and then do them
so well that people can't take
their eyes off you."
~Maya Angelou*

Chapter 5
Pearl #4 – Money Matters

As parents, we influence our children at an early age in matters relating to money. For example, making important decisions about what college to attend or what career to choose is solely based on how much it will cost or how much one will make can decrease the chances of a child reaching his or her full potential. Also, as parents, we can unwittingly instill a sense of fear in children around the belief that money is scarce and only certain people can increase their income.

I grew up always hearing my mother say, "The rich get richer, and the poor get poorer." Having a limiting set of beliefs around money such as the one above can actually cripple and hinder a child from pursuing their dreams.

I grew up in a home where money was always an issue. An issue which contributed to a significant portion of my anxiety over the years. Even today, I still struggle from time to time, either with not having enough money or having too much money. Both scenarios can cause me to have many sleepless nights.

It may seem obvious why not having enough money can cause sleepless nights, but why would a person be worried about having too much money in their account? Believe me, having too much money is almost as bad as not having enough money for a person like me who measures their worth in helping others.

In the early 1970s my parents bought our home in a neighborhood filled with other hardworking families. Both my parents came from small towns in the south and ventured out to big cities; my mother moved Boston and later to Chicago, and my father also moved to Chicago. In less than ten years they were married with three children and became homeowners in one of the largest metropolitan cities in the United States. I'm referring to the period, during the Nixon/Carter presidencies, the Black Panthers, Cesar Chavez, feminism, and the gas crisis.

Times were tough financially during the 70s. My mom and dad were average working-class people. My mother worked as a waitress and my father at O'Keefe and Merritt as a repairman.

One of my earliest memories around money was going to grocery shopping with my mother, and she always said in a very frustrating tone, "These groceries better not cost over a hundred dollars." Then I remember praying quietly, saying "God, please don't let the groceries cost more than a hundred dollars." Funny enough, the groceries, of course, came up to more than a hundred dollars and my mother cursed out loud about having to pay so much for these "Goddamned groceries." I remember feeling so uncomfortable and somewhat responsible for the groceries totaling over one hundred dollars.

Other memories I have are of my parents arguing about paying the bills. You see, in our home, my mother was in charge of paying all of the bills. My father would go to work, but when he got his paycheck he would give it all to my mother, and she would give him money for gas, cigarettes and his liquor each week. When we didn't have any extra money, he would complain it was because she paid the bills early instead of waiting an additional week. I remember the time I heard my father yelling, "That's my money! Those people can't tell me when and how much I need to pay them. I'll pay them when I want and how much I want to pay them. Don't send these payments in early!"

That exchange between my mom and dad went on for years while I was growing up. I was receiving all of these mixed messages around money, paying bills and spending money. As my siblings and I got older, the three of us got part-time jobs.

I worked at McDonald's when I turned 16 while my brother and sister worked at Foster's Freeze at the ages of 15 and 16. Having jobs meant we were able to take care of many of our own necessities and luxuries. For me especially, it meant I could exercise some independence over my life.

So, over the next five years, I concentrated more on working and paying my own bills and less on pursuing my dreams and keeping up with my school work. Working early at low paying jobs actually often hinders a child's motivation to attend college and pursue higher-paying jobs. Many get stuck in the low paying job rut for life, and it is harder to get out once you get in than for children whose parents tell them their job is "going to college."

The rich need their children as tax breaks until 26 and encourage and fund a focus on higher education.

Lacking the financial motivation to focus on my future career goals I chose to center my attention on my immediate goals of paying rent, making car payments, and having a full social life. Besides, my parents were actually proud of the fact that I had my own apartment, a nice car, and that I bought for myself and held down a job that allowed me to be independent.

However, I could hear my dreams calling me to refocus and recommit myself to fulfilling them. I remember when I told my father about my plans to go to college. He could not understand why I would quit a "good job" to set off to school. I tried to explain it to him and my mother, but in their minds, I was chasing a pipe dream, and I would be back in a few months working at the bank.

My mother would often say, "I'll never be rich, and I don't know anyone who has ever been rich." These are other examples of my family's set of limited beliefs surrounding money. As a parent, if you have any limiting beliefs around money, whether they are conscious or subconscious, addressing them will not only free you, but your children will be freed from these limiting set of beliefs, which can propel your family to a new level of financial freedom. And that is a fact.

According to an article posted in *Psychology Today*, here are some of the limiting beliefs around money that can repel wealth from us instead of propelling it to us.

1. It takes money to make money.
2. The rich get richer, and the poor get poorer.
3. Money is the root of all evil.
4. My financial success depends on the job market and the economy.
5. In climbing the ladder of success, you have to step on others on the way up.
6. You have to be in certain professions to make a lot of money.
7. Only a few actors (musicians, artists, writers, yadda yadda) ever make it to the top.

If we want our children to join this new generation of innovative, passionate, visionary, dynamic, risk-taking entrepreneurs, then we must change our thinking about money. Children most times emulate us and pick up energy from us, therefore if we are working hard at changing our belief system regarding money we can help launch them into a future where they are not fearful over money and not allowing money to dictate what goals they pursue. In that same article there is also a list of core beliefs of prosperous people:

1. The universe is abundant.
2. The universe wants ME to prosper.
3. All prosperity begins with belief.
4. Money is an abstraction.
5. Money is energy—and will appear as you really feel about it.
6. Money has no intelligence of its own.
7. Money will respond to the instructions I give it.
8. Money demands attention.

According to the author of my *Neuro-Linguistic Programming Training*, he teaches the four requisites of lasting change:

1. Get rid of negative emotions and beliefs, insert new positive beliefs.
2. Create a compelling future (goal setting).
3. Take action.
4. Remain focused on your desired outcome and reframe any obstacles to keep your unconscious moving forward.

"The goal of early childhood education should be to activate the child's own natural desire to learn."
~Maria Montessori

Chapter 6
Pearl #5 – Use Your Child's Interest as a Gateway to Learning

Maria Montessori pioneered what we now refer to as the Montessori Method. The Montessori Method was founded on Maria Montessori's educational philosophy. Her basic principle was to "follow the child." A Montessori classroom is carefully prepared to allow the child to work independently and allow for the joy of self-discovery. Teachers introduce materials and children are free to choose them, again and again, working and discovering, and ultimately mastering ideas. Then lessons are given, but the goal is for children to discover the answers by using the "auto-didactic," or "self-correcting" materials that are found only in Montessori classrooms.

As parents and guardians, we all want the same things for our children regardless of our level of income or education. We all want our children to be safe, healthy and happy. Unfortunately, not all of us know how to make sure our children receive it. As a teacher and administrator, I had no problem pointing out to parents how they need to make learning fun for the children. Parents should understand how much easier it would be on them if they incorporated play while teaching math, science or other subjects that their child may find difficult. As it is with most things, "easier said than done." I had to coach myself on how to get my own children excited about learning, and I will be honest, it was never easy.

Now, you know how they say, "doctors make the worst patients?" Well let's just say, teachers also make the worst students!

After years of attending Individual Education Plan (I.E.P.) meetings and facilitating 504 plan meetings, one would think I would be the best person to engage my special needs son who was now in eighth grade. Of course, I could be a supportive parent. As a matter of fact, as an assistant principal during these meetings, I listened to teachers give great suggestions to parents. I too had contributed many creative and original ideas to parents on how to engage with their child and get them excited about learning. However, when it came to practicing what I preached I could not, would not, or simply did not know how to apply it to my own child.

Notwithstanding, my son's first year of high school was extremely stressful for me. I took it upon myself to not only be his mother, but I was his teacher, counselor, and biggest advocate. The problem was… I was not advocating for him what was in his best interest. Instead, I was trying to get him to conform and learn the way I thought he should. I didn't want my son to use his learning disability as an excuse to slack off. I truly wanted to see him excel and thrive even with his deficits.

So, as most of you out there in Parentsville reading this book, I am sure you will relate to me when I say "I got on my son's last nerve and mine" during his first year of high school. It was tough, but I learned a lot about my son, his strengths and weaknesses. For example, I learned that if I used what he was already interested in, such as exotic animals and gaming he could pretty much learn anything and hold a halfway decent conversation. The key was tapping into his natural love for animals and using it as a "gateway to learning" other subjects.

Brian had been having difficulties in his English and U.S. History classes. So, since both subjects required the skills that he was the weakest in, these include writing, reading comprehension and speech and language acquisition, he was falling behind. He had two projects that were due, and if he did them well, he could raise his grades in both classes. This was a turning point for me as a parent.

At this point, I decided to listen to the advice I had given so many parents over the years and apply it to my son who was so desperately needing his mother to be loving and compassionate instead of cold and hard.

Brian opted to create a diorama of one of the Civil War Battles and the surrender at Appomattox Courthouse. I wish I had my cell phone ready to take a picture of his reaction when I told him to go upstairs and get his animals. "Get my animals," he squealed grinning from ear to ear. "Why?" he asked still smiling. We are going to use them for your project.

When he ran up the stairs, climbing two at a time, still smiling, all I could think of was, why hadn't I thought of this before? I am always telling parents how to use what their child is interested in, but in this case, I was doing the opposite. I was using what interested me in learning and trying to get him to learn the way I learned and to be interested in what I am interested in, which obviously did not work for us. At that moment I could hear Dr. Phil asking me, "And so how's that working for you?" Thinking of his famous question, all I could do was shake my head and say to myself, "It hasn't been really working for me."

Brian and I had so much fun working together on his project, and for the first time, I could see he was really excited about learning and knowing things about the Civil War. You may be asking yourself how did I do it? What was it about using the animals that got my son interested in learning about the Civil War? Well, all I can tell you is that you don't need a degree to make this happen. Instead, all you will need is some deep imagination and to connect with the intrinsic desires written upon your child's heart. Encourage each to become the person they are wired to be. Then it is easy.

For my son, I could connect him to anything using his love of animals. Once Brian came downstairs with the animals, I had him separate them into two categories, carnivores and herbivores (meat eaters and plant eaters). Next, I had him identify the animal from each group he would consider the leader of the pack. He identified the Lion as the leader of the carnivores, and the Gorilla as the leader of herbivores. Once he had identified the leaders, I asked him to suggest which one he thought should be Abraham Lincoln and which one should be Jefferson Davis. He identified Abraham Lincoln as the Lion and Jefferson Davis as the Gorilla. He did the same with the generals, labeling specific animals General Sherman, Lee, McClellan, and Grant. He did this for the Union and Confederate armies as well. We acted out a couple of battles using the animals. These were the notable Battle of Fort Sumter, Gettysburg, and Appomattox and, in addition, we reenacted the surrender of the Confederate Army and the ending of the Civil War. Brian can still discuss the Civil War to date, with confidence and accuracy and I know it is because I engaged him using his interest and not my interest.

The next project he needed to complete was for his English class. The assignment was to write a book that would be published and entered in a Young Authors contest. Again, writing is one of his weaknesses which is directly related to his learning disability, so I knew this would be quite tricky. Well, it just so happened my niece, Brian's favorite cousin, Kamani, who was a senior in high school, loved writing and was an English major. So, she agreed to help Brian with his book.

The first thing we did was have Brian come up with a topic. His topic was about animal rescue workers who traveled around the world trying to save exotic animals that were injured either by other animals or hunters. Then I learned that my son, who may have a problem articulating his thoughts orally or in writing, did not have a problem acting out and explaining his storyline to his cousin and myself. He also did not have a problem with the rescue workers getting injured or killed while they were on their mission to rescue these dangerous animals.

So, while he was acting out and explaining the scenarios using his rescue worker and animal figures, Kamani and I wrote his thoughts down as notes. We called this our brainstorming session. Once we had enough notes for a story, Kamani organized the notes and created an outline for Brian. Brian named the characters and was solely responsible for the story development, plot line, and pictures. Again, we had so much fun doing this and Brian and Kamani still talk about his book and how she helped him organize his thoughts.

Brian did the typing of the book, while Kamani and I helped him edit his book. We did this by reading the sentences he wrote out loud to him which allowed him to hear how it sounded. If he thought it sounded correct, we wouldn't change it. Whenever he thought it sounded correct and it wasn't correct, Kamani or myself would explain the correct tense or word that should be used and why.

The entire weekend was one of those great parenting and teachable moments for me. Listening to my son was a lesson I learned one of the most valuable lessons as a parent and an educator, one in which I made a point to practice more with my son and students. Pairing students in the classrooms or siblings in the home to support each other combines empowerment by helping others with connecting to the heart desires of the child.

Of course, I'm also human, and a few years later when Brian was a junior in high school and obsessed with video games, I would lecture him on how he was wasting his time with video games. I compared my love for watching old TV movies and how I actually increased my vocabulary and other skills that I could apply. So, I looked at Brian, (you all know the look we give as parents when we believe we are making a point with our children), and I asked him with an air of arrogance, "What is it you learn from playing video games that you can actually use?" He looked at me and replied matter-of-fact, "Strategy." Playing video games teaches you strategy. He then went on to explain how this strategy helps him with his studies, work at the zoo, and other extracurricular activities. I had to pick my face up off the floor after he so respectfully checked me.

So, there you have it, parents. Our children are pretty intelligent, and they know a lot more than we give them credit for. The key is finding out what they are passionate about and using it to get them excited about learning. These strategies are more effective when applied early in a child's life before they have built up a wall and are resistant to learning because they lack some skills that are necessary. And may have as well developed a great interest in some other ways of learning that suits their interest. So, you have to spend less time focusing your attention on their deficits (unless you are working to improve them) and more time focusing your attention on the things they are good at.

Children like adults love to be praised and told they are doing a good job. So, it is very necessary that you find ways to give your child words of encouragement and remember, for every criticism you should follow it up with at least two compliments. This will stand as an effective means of balancing out what your child is hearing and internalizing. According to *Parent News*, a child who is constantly criticized can become insecure, . *"However, when parents criticize, it has the opposite effect; it actually demotivates and discourages their children. Criticism actually squashes any feeling a child may have in trying something new, and it results in them feeling alienated from their parents. Criticized children end up feeling angry, worthless, unloved and undeserving, and their self-esteem drops. Around and around it goes. It's a vicious circle that parents keep alive with their continual hurtful criticism."*

"If a child can't learn the way we teach, maybe we should teach the way they learn."
~ Ignacio Estrada

Chapter 7
Pearl #6 – Diagnosis and A New Way of Learning

I talk a lot about teaching in Atlanta, Moreno Valley, Clarkston, and Apple Valley. However, my very first year of teaching was in Charlotte, North Carolina.

I had just graduated from the Harvard Graduate School of Education, and I was offered a job right on the spot at our job fair. Well not really on the spot, as I was offered first right of refusal so, I had an opportunity to go in and meet with the principal for an interview and then I was given the first right of refusal.

Credentialed in Social Science, not Special Education I had not been trained to work with students who required special accommodations. My understanding of students with learning disabilities was limited to my experiences as a young student myself.

In junior high school, I remember there was this classroom where students with disabilities received their daily instruction. The students in this classroom were mainly students with severe learning, physical, and medical problems such as Cerebral Palsy and Down's Syndrome. Although my memories are vague I recall these students had very low IQ's or as we called them, were "very slow." Also, there was usually some type of physical characteristic to indicate they required special attention in a separate classroom.

It is important to point out I attended high school and junior high school in the early to mid-80s, an entire decade earlier than when I began teaching. There had been a number of changes in Special Education in the last decade that I was unaware of and unprepared for.

In 1996, as a first-year teacher at Providence High School, I taught three classes for gifted students in civics and economics, and two general classes of the same subjects. In all classes, I had at least one to two students who were on an Individual Education Plan (I.E.P.).

Typically, these were students who were previously diagnosed with Attention Deficit Disorder (ADD), or Attention Deficit Hyperactivity Disorder

(ADHD), or some type of visual or processing delay. The majority were all very high functioning students who maintained solid A or B grades.

Therefore, as I began to receive notifications that required my presence at their annual I.E.P. meetings I was perplexed. My limited knowledge of students with disabilities did not match up with the students I had in my classes. My memories were of students who were mentally slow and/or physically impaired. The young lady I received my first meeting notification for did not fit the image I had in my mind. She was a physically fit, attractive Caucasian female with thick and wavy light brown hair and blue eyes. She was quiet and studious and nothing in her work ethic or work product indicated she had any type of learning disability.

In the meeting, her mother, a professional woman in the banking industry, was well versed on her daughter's educational rights. She confidently relayed information regarding accommodations that her daughter should be receiving. During the meeting, she specifically shared with me how her daughter was getting lost in my oral explanations and directions. Perhaps in addition to oral, I could also write important information and instructions on the board. This adjustment would also serve other students in addition to her daughter who may not be auditory learners but are instead visual learners.

Aha! A light bulb went on in my mind. I thought to myself, that's funny I am a visual learner. Why had I not realized this and incorporated this strategy into my teaching? I also realized it was because while I may be a visual learner I am an auditory teacher as my biggest strength in teaching is storytelling. I am at my best when I am explaining history through storytelling.

Besides, in my Masters Program at Harvard, we focused primarily on how to motivate and engage "at risk" students. At the time, there was an immense amount of literature on the achievement gap and drop-out rates among certain minority groups.

To clarify, it is not my intention to give the impression that in 1995-96 Harvard was not giving any priority to ensuring teachers were prepared for students with disabilities. However, at the time my focus was centered around "at-risk" students, especially since at the time I was carrying out my student teaching duties at one of the lowest performing schools in Boston, Massachusetts. Dorchester High had so many low-performing students that even the students referred to the school as "Dumbchester."

The students were well aware the school was on life support and most people wanted to pull the plug. I can recall one day several months into my student teaching seeing a student who had not shown up to my class in a few days, standing in the hallway. I asked him why he had not been to class. Sadly he replied, "It's not you Ms. Morrow. I checked out a long time ago, long before you got here."

My intent was to highlight and give context as to why special education strategies were not on my radar during my student teaching or Masters preparation due to the immediate need of the students I was currently serving.

After that meeting, I immediately adjusted my delivery method in all of my classes. The following morning when I arrived in class, I wrote the directions on the board and next I explained to them orally and checked for understanding with the students.

The experience I gained from the parents and students at that I.E.P. meeting has enhanced the way in which I deliver instruction and manage my classes. I make it a priority to incorporate a variety of learning modalities in my lessons to maximize participation from all students. A few years later strategies I learned took on a more personal meaning for me as I would soon discover my son had a learning disability.

In 1999 my son was born four weeks early which at that time was not considered premature. Yet I immediately noticed he was not developing at the rate his sister had developed six years earlier. He had not mastered latching on to my breasts for his feedings which I later learned was due to a delay in the development of his sucking muscles. Other things such as crawling and walking were also delayed. Finally, at age three when he was still unable to talk, but instead pointed at things he wanted or needed, I decided it was time to find out what was going on. Thanks to my teaching experience at Providence High School in Charlotte, North Carolina, an upscale area where new money resided, I could get a pretty good idea of what needed to be done.

I said to my husband, "Look, if rich people can get help for their children and benefit from supports and resources, we can do the same. Why should our child struggle needlessly in school because we are ashamed or embarrassed about him being labeled? The parents I met with who lived in gated communities and drove Hummers, Mercedes and Jaguars certainly were not embarrassed." He agreed and left it up to me to pursue the testing and evaluation for our son.

There is overwhelming data that confirms African-American males and Latino males are overrepresented in Special Education classes. In addition, poverty plays a significant role in the over-identification of students with learning disabilities. Understanding the statistics and the stigma attached I felt strongly that the pros out-weighed the cons, and I made an appointment to have our son tested. He was diagnosed with Developmental Delay and Speech and Language Delay at three and a half years old. So began my son Brian's educational journey in the world of Free and Appropriate Education (FAPE). I received a crash course on the Individuals with Disabilities Act, Special Education meetings, advocates, testing, accommodations, and modifications. I became overwhelmed by the reality of his diagnosis and the fact this would be our new normal for the rest of our lives.

As challenging as it has been for us over the years, the sad truth is there are many parents who will not have their children tested. There are a number of reasons why, but mainly because of the stigma they believe is attached to an identification of a learning disability. As a result, each year there are scores of children that go unidentified and do not receive the sources and resources that could actually help them succeed academically. There are also a number of parents that fear their child may not get the education they deserve, may be neglected educationally, or teachers may simply fail to accommodate them. Regrettably, I cannot categorically state nothing like this will ever occur, because it had happened to my son more than once while he was in school.

I acknowledge the fact that most teachers choose to go into Special Education because they have a true passion for educating students with "different abilities." Although there are the few who do not have the drive, commitment, or compassion to be a Special Education teacher, most truly desire to help. Still, teaching special needs children is daunting and exhausting. Teaching is no different from any other profession where you have people that cut corners, except in education when a teacher cuts corners it's our children who are negatively impacted which could take years to counteract. So, it is important for parents to make sure their child has a quality teacher who cares and works hard.

I was faced with this situation on more than one occasion when my son was in school. However, the most egregious incident occurred when my son was in eighth grade and attending one of the schools in the same district where I was employed as an administrator. Before taking the job as an administrator, I taught U.S. History to high school students for eleven years. When this incident occurred, I was the current assistant principal over the Social Science department.

My son would bring home completed assignments with a passing grade that initially pleased me; however, when I read the questions and his answers, I suddenly realized he was not actually answering the questions. All he was doing was rewriting the questions and his teacher would give him full credit, not noticing the writing was a repetition of the question.

Once I realized this was not an anomaly but instead a common practice, I was livid! I was not one of those teachers or parents who believed it was ok to pass a student just because he was not a discipline problem and he appeared to be confused. Instead of working with my child to ensure he understood certain concepts she chose to slap ten points on his paper and move him along. Up to this point, Brian and I had been accustomed to teachers who held him accountable and responsible for doing the work correctly and turning it in. Sometimes this meant his teachers worked with him individually and sometimes it meant I worked with him, but he was responsible for learning the material. I was so upset I decided to speak with some of the Special Education teachers on my campus to get ideas about what type of accommodations and modifications I could recommend to the teacher to support Brian's learning. I did not want to tear into her, assuming that as a veteran teacher with years of experience she should already know the appropriate accommodations to give. Next, I requested a copy of his psychological report to make sure the accommodations supported his specific learning disability. The accommodation that was rooted in "he doesn't have to do the work, or I'll accept whatever work he turns in" was not going to fly with me. NOT ON MY WATCH! This phrase became my mantra while my son was in school.

Finally, armed with the knowledge of his precise deficits along with the appropriate accommodations and modifications, I scheduled a meeting with his assistant principal (he taught Brian in 5th grade in another school district), special education resource teacher/case carrier, social science teacher, English teacher and counselor.

On the day of the meeting, I was calm and able to conduct myself in a professional manner. I had had two weeks to process the information and seek support from teachers on my campus. I handed the teachers a copy of his psychological report which I was surprised to learn they had not been provided with a copy before the meeting. I discussed the possible accommodations and modifications they could make to ensure Brian's future success. The teachers were not resistant at all, in fact, they welcomed the information and were appreciative I had brought suggestions with me.

This experience taught me a number of valuable lessons, the main one being as a parent of a child with a learning disability there is more to it than simply the designation of Special Education. It is important for parents to understand the learning disability, the appropriate accommodations and/or modifications and being able to effectively communicate requests and know how to hold everyone accountable for carrying them out.

It's not easy being the parent of a child with special needs. It is hard, frustrating, time-consuming work. But, it is work that is necessary for a child to have any chance of succeeding academically in life.

"There is no more powerful advocate for children than a parent armed with information and options."
~ Rod Paige

Chapter 8
Pearl #7 Be Your Child's Hero

Dr. Rita Pierson said it best in her famous 2013 Ted Talk. "Every kid needs a champion." Although the audience was mostly made up of educators and the topics in her speech were geared toward teachers, it is still a topic everyone involved with children can draw inspiration from.

Most parents, including me, will agree with Dr. Pierson that: "Every child needs a champion." However, a number of parents I have worked with throughout the years strongly believe they are their child's champion. But, there are a number of parents who want to be their child's champion, who do not feel they have the knowledge nor the skill to advocate in the best interest of their child.

These are common questions and statements frustrated parents have shared with me over the years:

> "How can I fight for my child's rights if I barely graduated from high school? I didn't go to college. I can barely read. I have a hard time speaking English. How do I even know the school is doing everything they should be doing for my child? I feel like the school has all the power and I have none, so I just stay quiet even if I don't think they are not doing what is best for my child."

When I hear parents verbally express these feelings, I share one of my favorite lines from a Tyler Perry movie: "You hold all the cards," referring to the power every parent holds regarding their child's education and schooling. However, I know from experience it's not power parents lack, it's knowledge and confidence. As we all know, knowledge is power and confidence in your knowledge is what earns you respect.

This chapter will give you three key easy to implement strategies and resources to help you gain the knowledge and confidence you can immediately begin using at your children's school meetings, conferences, and other interactions with faculty and staff.

1. Form Parent-Teacher Relationships

First and foremost, establish a relationship early on with your child's school teachers. This is especially helpful if you already know that your child has some academic and/or behavior issues. You are letting the teacher and other staff members know you are well aware of your child's specific needs without giving excuses. As educators, we prefer parents are upfront with us regarding their children's particular issues.

My first year as an administrator after freshman orientation, I had a number of parents who approached me to discuss their children's issues going into high school. One in particular I remember was the wife of a former administrator and the adoptive mother to two boys, one a junior and one a freshman.

She immediately told me how she appreciated my positive approach, and how I welcomed the opportunity to work with parents before any real problems arose. She followed me to my office where we talked about her son's previous behavior issues in elementary and middle school.

This lady had no illusions about her son or what he was capable of. What she needed was someone at the school who understood her child was not "bad" or "unredeemable," but that he needed some consistent intervention, accountability, patience, and nurturing.

Mrs. Wilson and I sat down and she was very frank with me about her son's past behaviors and how they were a problem for her son. She told me about how he would shut down or blow up if he felt singled out or attacked. She shared with me that if he felt safe in sharing he would admit the truth instead of telling a lie, which he often did out of fear of abandonment.

During that conversation, she shared personal details regarding her son, his issues and their commitment to working with him to see him succeed. She then said to me, "Call anytime for any reason. There is nothing too small or petty when it comes to our son." I agreed and I thought to myself, this woman most certainly knows her son better than me, she is the expert on him, therefore, I absolutely need to listen to her and follow her advice regarding her son.

During the next few years, I developed a personal relationship with the young Wilson boy, and this information helped build the basis to provide the support he needed. This included regular check-ins with him, his teacher and parents. I would often visit his classes and take a seat near him, questioning him about the lesson and noting when he was off task. The young Wilson boy was not the only student with whom I developed a personal relationship. I repeated this strategy with nearly half of the class of 2012. As a result, parents trusted me when I called them with negative reports. My family admin team nicknamed me the "nurturer" because of the patience, compassion, and amount of attention I would expend on students, particularly the students that others had written off.

Parents, start the conversation with teachers and administrators. It can begin with an unguarded honest conversation regarding your child and their areas of strengths and weaknesses. Being open and honest and following up with your child's teachers and administrators will go a long way in their school career.

If you call them and do not receive a reply, email them or send a note. If you still do not receive a reply, or the feedback you had hoped for, contact their school administrator, and if the administrator is not responsive, contact the principal's boss.

There's something I learned many years ago at the start of my career, the squeaky wheel really does get the oil. Meaning, you have got to speak up and make some noise if you want the "grease" for your child.

Remember this: You hold all the cards. You're the parent and you have the power as long as you understand that power and how to use it.

There are appropriate timelines and chain of commands that must be followed. For example, if you contact your child's teacher on a Monday, you should wait a reasonable period of time before you can expect the teacher to get back to you. Forty-eight hours is a reasonable turnaround time to expect a return call or email from your child's teacher.

Also, find out how much time your district requires to resolve complaints that have been filed before calling to follow up. Most districts require anywhere from 30-60 days to resolve a complaint. Also, be sure to have a suggestion or solution for your child's teacher before calling them. The details of the solution can be ironed out between you and the teacher when you meet.

The objective is to intervene before you get to the point where you are at a loss and have no idea what to do regarding your child.

Second, know your child's rights and your rights as a parent. This information can be located on your school district's website, parent and student handbook, and school website. If your school has more than one hundred students that speak a language other than Spanish, the school is required to send the information home in that language. Should a parent require an interpreter it is the district's responsibility to ensure the parent has an interpreter at meetings or other school functions to increase involvement, and right now you may be asking yourself, where can I get this information about my rights and child's rights?

Many parents who may not have the language skills or reading skills may not feel skilled enough to read and interpret the information that is located on their school and/or district's website. One of things I'm most proud of is the parent empowerment center I envisioned becoming a reality where with the hard work of the parents, staff, students, and consultant we were able to implement a model center that involved parents. Our center became a place where parents could come to be educated on district, state, and federal policies and laws. Parents were given the tools and support to advocate for their children at school and district meetings. Parents learned how to navigate the school district's website for information on school, district, state, and federal policies. Parents were invited to workshops and training conducted by local organizations, various non-profit organizations and the county office of education. Our parents began to gain confidence in speaking up for their children at district board meetings, school meetings, and other training and workshops.

Parent involvement in their child's education is so important that it has been part of the US Department of Education's policy going back as far as 1965 with the Elementary and Secondary Education Act. Although these policies have evolved over the years, the primary objective of involving parents from underserved communities remains a significant strand of the policy. It ensures equity and that the school has an on-going conversation to understand the local needs of the communities they serve.

Here is an excerpt of the Elementary and Secondary Education Act, specifically related to the role of schools in parental involvement, (ESEA), Title I, Part A, Section 1118(2)(e);

> 2. Written Policy - *Each local educational agency that receives funds under this part shall develop jointly with, agree on with, and distribute to, parents of participating children a written parent involvement policy. The policy shall be incorporated into the local educational agency's plan developed under Section 1112, establish the agency's expectations for parent involvement, and describe how the agency will:*
>
> e. *Conduct, with the involvement of parents, an annual evaluation of the content and effectiveness of the parental involvement policy in improving the academic quality of the schools served under this part, including identifying barriers to greater participation by parents in activities authorized by this section (with particular attention to parents who are economically disadvantaged, disabled, have limited English proficiency, have limited literacy, or are of any racial or ethnic minority background), and use the findings of such evaluation to design strategies for more effective parental involvement, and to revise if necessary the parental involvement policies described in this section.*

For parents who are struggling with communicating with their child's school teachers and need support there are parent empowerment organizations, advocacy groups, and English Learner Advocacy groups springing up around cities to serve underserved communities.

In Hartford, Connecticut there is an organization called the Sheff Movement which is a coalition of parents, educators, faith leaders and community activists members committed to ensuring implementation of the Sheff vs. O'Neil case in Hartford public schools. The organization is under the leadership of co-chairs Jim Boucher and Elizabeth Horton Sheff one of the plaintiffs in the "landmark civil rights case that seeks to prepare all children to live and prosper in an increasingly diverse, globally connected world."

Another notable organization is Memphis Lift started by parents and grandparents to educate, empower and engage parents from high poverty areas to "raise awareness of inequity and demand high-quality education through choice and competition."

Lastly, parents who are concerned about their child's learning ability or behavior issues which require more than the customary interventions should begin to ask how they can help their child and/or who can they speak to about getting help for their child.

2. Test for Learning Disabilities

When in doubt, test to find out if your child has a learning disability.

In my years as an administrator and the parent of a child with a learning disability, I advise parents to be open to the possibility of getting their child tested if no other reason than to rule out a learning disability.

Many parents are unaware they can request in writing that their child be considered for testing to determine if there is a learning disability or not. The request by the parent must be made in writing to the school, and once the school receives the request, they have sixty days to comply with the request.

Many parents believe that simply discussing the possibility of a learning disability with their child's teacher or counselor is enough to get the ball rolling and are frustrated when nothing gets done. A request for evaluation must be made in writing, dated and signed by the parent or guardian who holds the educational rights for the child for whom an evaluation is being requested.

Once a child is evaluated, parents meet with an IEP (Individual Educational Plan) team to discuss the results of the evaluation and if a new placement in specialized classes is recommended. Parental signature and agreement are needed to place the child in special education and the parent can request to keep their child in the mainstream with modifications from regular teachers who are notified of the student's learning disability.

Parents should listen carefully to the teacher's observations and comments to see if this is a possibility for their child or if it will be too hard and a special needs class that is easier is perhaps a better option for their child.

It is necessary throughout the process to remain patient, confident, and persistent. Listen and realize that ultimately, the parent has the power to decide what is best for their child and doesn't have to go along with the biases and pressures of educators.

Present yourself as an agreeable parent, yet make them aware that you are familiar with your child's rights and responsibilities as well as yours, and the school's rights and responsibilities.

However, most importantly, be prepared to move up the chain of command if your child's rights are not being honored.

Communicate what you want and why you think it is best for your child. Make sure you keep your child in the conversation, especially with teenagers, and do not let the adults make all the decisions without an older child's input.

3. Educate Yourself as a Parent

Empowering your child begins with empowering yourself, which is a task that requires you to commit to the process.

There is a time commitment and a willingness to be open to new information and a new way of communicating with your child, teachers, and other staff involved in his/her educational journey.

Parenting can be one of the toughest jobs you will ever have, but it is the most rewarding of any job you will have in your life.

Read and know your rights. Have others read aloud to you if you cannot read.

I hope some of you are listening to this on audio CD and learning no matter what your own educational and reading level is. With modern day technology, we all can access information more easily and become better educated on our rights.

*"Taking care of yourself is part of
taking care of your kids."
~CafeMom*

Chapter 9
Pearl #8 – The Importance of Self-Care

I am not unlike many parents who choose to sacrifice their health, time, and finances in the name of giving the best for their children. We all sacrifice and give what we wish our parents could have given for us. We envision a life free of struggles, worries and bad times. In fact, we often quote how our children are supposed to climb higher than us, be more successful than us, and have a lot more money than us. Which leads us to work harder, spend more and for lack of a fancier word, drive ourselves crazy trying to do and be everything for our children to ensure their success.

Sadly, this superhero syndrome can become too much to handle if it is not reigned in, which is exactly what happened to me. After so many years of being Superwoman, Super Mom, Super Teacher, and Super Boss, my life as I knew it came crashing down on me because while I was taking care of everyone else's needs, I neglected to care for my own.

It's funny, in all of the years I watched Oprah on her talk show discuss the importance of self-care and the damaging effects of what could happen if we failed to take time to satisfy our needs, I still continued on my self-sacrificing road of self-destruction. I had the superhero parent syndrome. I listened as Oprah, as well as other guests, explained why it is not selfish to take care of yourself and why it is vital for us to do so.

Airplane attendants instruct every parent to place the oxygen mask over their own face first and then on their child. My father tried to teach me to save myself first also as a child, which my selfless nature questioned as impossible.

My father would conduct random fire drills which often occurred in the middle of the night. He would wake us all up and force us to flee the house in whatever clothing we were wearing and meet in the backyard. These drills were always timed to see how long it would take us to get out of the house and to a safe area. Once the drill was concluded my father would debrief us on the things we did right and the things that still needed improvement. I remember him specifically looking at me and saying, "Self-preservation is the first law of man. If this house catches on fire you have to run out and get to safety. You cannot wait for Kam or go back to the house to get her." Any fireman will tell you never run into a burning building!

At the time, I remember challenging my father's line of thought by pointing out to him that as the oldest child there was no way I could leave my little sister in a burning house and not try to go back to save her. I distinctly remember him looking at me with fear in his eyes and saying, "That's what I'm afraid of. If you run back in the house to try to save Kam, then I lose both of you. You both will burn up in a fire." Of course, as a child, I thought my father was way out of line for advising me to take care of myself first. This went against everything I believed in as a teenage girl. How in the world could he possibly say something like that to me? I was the oldest, a natural caregiver, there was no doubt in my mind that I would go back in to save her.

It is most parents' instinct to want to lay down their life for their child, but we have to realize the parent must take care of themselves to save the child.

After so many years spent working with students, parents and other educators while at the same time raising two of my three children as a single working mother it dawned on me how little I put myself first. How rarely I took the time out to focus on my needs and in contrast how often I would rearrange my schedule and finances to accommodate my children's needs and wants.

I rationalized that my children needed to come first, especially since I was both mother and father since their fathers both lived in different states from us.

I had myself convinced that as a parent it was my duty to ensure my children had everything (within reason) they desired. I had envisioned a particular lifestyle for us, and I was not going to let the lack of a second parent, my son's special needs, or my demanding job change the vision I had in any way.

After several trips to the Emergency Room and a number of missed follow up appointments, I finally hit my bottom. I was irritable, gaining weight, forgetful (they call it brain fog) and having shortness of breath and heart palpitations. I was I hospitalized and strongly encouraged (ordered) to seek treatment.

During this time, I learned a valuable lesson. You have to listen to your body and it will tell you exactly what you need to do, and if not, it will send signals which will force you to deal with the issue. This is what happened to me.

I was experiencing shortness of breath, fatigue and other asthmatic symptoms. I went to Urgent Care, and I was told by the treating physician I was not having an asthma attack I was having an anxiety attack. I consider myself a strong independent woman which meant I had no time to be having an anxiety attack.

Again, I missed my follow up appointment, and I did not take the prescribed medication. Less than two weeks later I was back in the Urgent Care, this time I thought I had Shingles. In my twenties I had them, and I remembered they were extremely painful. I had awakened with severe pains on my back and arms. Therefore, I concluded I must have Shingles. However, on this day it was my primary physician who I had been deliberately avoiding by going to Urgent Care who appeared. As she walked through the door, I felt the blood drain from my face and I began to feel guilty for never having followed up with any of my appointments.

She examined me as I shared my concerns and she very calmly explained I was, in fact, having an anxiety attack. She reminded me of my diagnosis of Severe Anxiety and Major Depression. She also reminded me that my blood pressure was high and since I never seemed to make it back for my follow up readings she would be prescribing me all of the necessary medications. I inquired about the severe pain I was feeling, and she informed me, Anxiety will mimic other illnesses if you do not treat it.

In my mind, all I could think is our bodies are very powerful. I wish I could say I listened to my doctor's sage advice, got my prescription filled, and everything turned out great for me. Unfortunately, I still did not listen to my doctor or my body which is how I wound up being hospitalized as I said earlier.

A year later after starting and stopping my medications and continuing to place everyone's needs ahead of my own and attempt to live up to these exceedingly high expectations I placed on myself, I finally broke. I don't wish this emotional or physical pain on anyone.

During my major depressive episode as it is now referred to as, I could hear my father's voice saying, "Self-preservation is the first law of man." Through counseling over the next few months, I came to understand my father was not wrong. All those years ago, what I thought were the ravings of a madman, I learned in my counseling group, this was very sound advice, and my dad was indeed a man ahead of his time. I had a hero complex.

In the group, our counselor used being on an airplane as an example of putting oneself first. Annie, although not her real name, reminded us that when flying, the directions given to passengers in the event the cabin begins to lose pressure and the oxygen masks drop down are, "You should first put on your own mask, and then assist small children." Well gee, is that what my father was trying to say all those years ago?

Not that I would have listened even if he put it that way. In my mind, I still would have thought that would have been an act of selfishness. I learned that destroying myself would leave me helpless to help anyone else and that I really did need to take care of me.

It took a breakdown for me to realize this. Hopefully, reading this will help you to take pro-active self-care before it reaches that point as it did for me.

However, humbling as it was having gone through a breakdown, it is now clear to me that there is definitely some validity to this line of thinking that if I do not take care of me, I am no good to anyone. So, finally, it's time for me to begin listening to my father's voice in my mind and pay attention to the recommendations being made by the caring, compassionate counselor who clearly knows what she is talking about.

Any experienced healthcare provider will tell you why it is important to practice self-care and what the consequences are when you fail to do so. Over the past thirty years, a number of parent groups, magazines, and also various blogs have been pointing out how critical it is for parents to practices self-care and why practicing self-care is the opposite of being selfish.

There are plenty of reasons why it is important for parents to put themselves first, but perhaps the greatest reason of all is if you hope to continue to give your children the best care you can give to them, you have to give the best care to yourself as well. You cannot give of yourself if you do not have anything left of yourself to give.

Suicide is on the rise and our pride and ignorance of our own needs for too long with the hero syndrome is sometimes a cause of this. We all need to be humble enough to seek help when we need it and take care of ourselves. For some of us, it is harder than for others.

There are a number of ways as parents we can practice self-care and most of them we can do for free or for a low cost. Here are a few examples I learned while attending group therapy sessions.

Diet and exercise are the number one recommendations by all healthcare professionals, counselors, and most anyone for relieving stress. Making small changes to your diet and exercise routine can add years to your life withan added bonus of decreasing weight from your waistline. Changing your diet does not have to be drastic.Instead start by adding fresh fruit and vegetables to your diet.

Listen here, this an apple a day we have all heard will keep the doctor away. I grew up with a mother that believed in healthy eating and cardio exercises. She would make large fresh salads loaded with fruits and vegetables. Her desserts would not contain any sugar or fattening oils. Instead, she would find recipes that called for using applesauce instead of cooking oil and fresh or frozen fruits instead of sugar.

Each day she would take her thirty-minute walk around the neighborhood, and she also employed other tactics such as parking far away from her destination to force the extra walking and taking the stairs instead of the elevator.

My mom would also say to me that I should never I allow my children to stress me out. "I never let you kids stress me out. Kim, you are going to have a heart attack or stroke worrying so much about making these kids happy," my mom warned me more than once.

Boy, I wish I would have listened to her as she was most undoubtedly a wise woman.

Of course, my doctor has repeated to me the same words as my mother many times. Diet and exercise are key to a long healthy life. Reduce or eliminate caffeine, alcohol, foods high in sodium, sugar, and fat to include all of the good fried foods which I love so much.

And as for the exercise, try walking at least thirty minutes a day, dancing, riding a bike, hiking, yoga all of the things that you enjoy and are fun. And look fun.

Sometimes, exercising can feel more like a chore or as a counselor I used to work with explained to her students, there are "I have to do's" like laundry and dishes and there are "I want to do's" like playing school sports or going to dances. However, if you choose activities that are fun for you they will feel less like "have to do's" and more like "want to do's."

Other stress-relieving activities are journaling, crafting, drawing and painting, woodworking, coloring, blowing bubbles, meditation. and listening to soothing music. During therapy, I began to tap into my creative side which I had neglected during my years of raising children and working as an educator. I rediscovered my love for writing and creating stories, which has led me to go back to writing fiction stories and, of course, this non-fiction piece. I also tapped into my love of arts and crafts.

I wish I were a talented artist with a knack for painting and drawing like Da Vinci, Matisse or Faith Ringgold, but I was not blessed with that gift. My gift was in storytelling, writing and building meaningful relationships with people. A gift that I am learning to balance.

Balance is what we as parents must learn. It's essential we learn to balance our responsibilities as parents, employees or employers reconciling responsibilities with being our own creative person. It's important that our children not only learn from us how to be successful and earn a good living; it is just as important that we teach our children how to take care of themselves and play and enjoy life.

Children learn from what we do, not what we say. If all they see is us working hard and neglecting our physical and mental health, they will learn to do the same. We will be raising children who will suffer from all sorts of physical and mental ailments if we continue as we are with failing to put ourselves first. My daddy said it best all those years ago. "Self-preservation is the first law of man." I regret it took me so long to listen to his words of wisdom.

✓ **To Do List**
Keep Track of Each Item Completed.

1.

2.

3.

4.

5.

6.

7.

8.

9.

10.

Date

Journal Entry

> An informed parent or caregiver becomes empowered, and empowerment can lead to the best care for our children.
>
> — Charisse Montgomery

Chapter 10
Extra Pearls

As I wrap up this book, I would like to leave you with some practical knowledge you can begin to immediately apply toward a child's academic success.

The first of these pearls of wisdom is: make a commitment to [1]*continual improvement*. Creating improvement goals is much more effective than simply setting long-term goals. In fact, according to Graeme Turner in the article, Successful People Don't Set Goals, "[2]defining goals defines your limitations."

Instead, studies in various fields such as business, technology, and healthcare endorse the notion of committing to growing as an individual. Encouraging children to set measurable and attainable improvements in various areas of their lives proves more successful and leaves little room to lose motivation than trying to adhere to long term goals. [3]They look at what they can do each day to make a small improvement that, over time, adds up. In fact, a 1% improvement, over 68 days means you will be 100% better than you were yesterday. Children need to build routines that build toward goals for themselves at an early age. This is vital to their long-term success.

> Dear Reader, my hope is that my book is only the beginning of your journey to empowering your child to maximize their full potential and still find time to replenish your soul. I have listed a few of the websites I frequently visit to gain inspiration when trying to keep my students engaged and encouraged.

---

[1] Why Successful people Don't Set Goals and You Shouldn't Either, Graeme Turner
[2] Ibid
[3] Ibid

Online Resources

Americans with Disabilities Act ADA
https://www.ada.gov

Autism Speaks
https://www.autismspeaks.org

Goal Setting Basics
http://www.goalsettingbasics.com/goal-setting-for-kids.html

Code.org
https://code.org/

Growth Mindset
https://www.mindsetworks.com/science/

Home School Connections
http://www.homeschool-connections.com/

Individuals with Disabilities Education Act IDEA
https://sites.ed.gov/idea

Kiddie Matters
https://www.kiddiematters.com/teaching-children-how-to-set-goals-and-use-a-vision-board/

National Alliance on Mental Illness
https://www.nami.org

Parents Magazine
www.parentsmagazine.com

Autism Speaks
https://www.autismspeaks.org

Partnership for 21st Century Learning
https://www.p21.org

Reach Institute Parent Empowerment Program
https://thereachinstitute.org/services/for-healthcare-organizations/staff-training/parent-empowerment

Sheff Movement
https://sheffmovement.org

Very Well Mind
https://www.verywellmind.com/tips-to-reduce-stress-3145195

Works Cited

Greiner, LaDonna, 21 Reasons to Say Thank You, September 7, 2017
https://www.21reasonstosaythankyou.com/blog/category/grateful-kids/

Montessori, Maria, https://www.mariamontessori.com/

Sisgold, Steve, Psychology Today. June 4, 2013. Date July 25, 2018
https://www.psychologytoday.com/us/blog/life-in-body/201306/limited-beliefs

Waters, Laura, Education Post, May 7, 2015, Date August 1, 2018
http://www.educationpost.org/teach-the-way-children-learn-one-mothers-gratitude-for-a-teacher/

United States Department of Education, https://www.ed.gov/admins/comm/parents/parentinvolve/index.html

www.ingramcontent.com/pod-product-compliance
Lightning Source LLC
Chambersburg PA
CBHW051410290426
44108CB00015B/2225